PRAYERS TO SURVIVE WARS THAT LAST

(POEMS)

CHIELOZONA EZE

PRAYERS TO SURVIVE WARS THAT LAST. Copyright ©
2017 by Chielozona Eze.

Publisher's information, address:
Cissus World Press, P.O. Box 240865, Milwaukee, WI 53224
www.cissusworldpressbooks.com

CWP ISBN: 978-0-9978689-4-4
First published in the U.S.A by Cissus World Press

First Edition

CISSUS WORLD PRESS BOOKS.

Distributor:
African Books Collective
Website: http://www.africanbookscollective.com/
Email: orders@africanbookscollective.com

Prayers to Survive Wars that Last

Dedication

The millions who have been forgotten.
I lay these wreaths on your tombs wherever they may be.
Take them and forgive us.

July 6, 1967 - Janurary15, 1970

Contents

he remembers other people in pain

he just wants to dance

Preface
by *Chris Abani*

Chielozona Eze is unusual in the tradition of recent West African and Nigerian poetics. With the exception perhaps of amu nnadi, most Nigerian poets focus on the rallying call of protest, politics, and nation. They attempt to lay bare the difficult things at the heart of public and social mechanisms, institutions, and interactions in language calculated to both harangue power and muster a shift in the average citizen's relationship to nation, and in this way compel citizenship with all the responsibility that attends it. This is neither a good nor a bad thing. I merely point this out because of the shift in perspective and aesthetic focus that Eze's work offers us.

Eze chooses a different direction, honing in first on the personal and the struggle of the individual to make meaning, and to forge a language to contain that meaning in a way that always allows the lyric turn to happen, always allowing uncertainty to live at the heart of things, like the trickster we know as Esu in Yoruba, or Agwu in Igbo. This offers a new and more nuanced way to open up the larger issues at the heart of a culture.

This new approach to the lyric tradition with the Nigerian and larger African poetic context and conversation is new and radical. It creates an intimacy with the reader and allows for an audience, no matter how close or far to the historical material at the heart to the work, to connect in more explicit ways than in the work of earlier poets. His opening poem, "The Art of Loving What's Imperfect," is Ars Poetica, artistic manifesto, a deep personal philosophical search for self and yet paradoxically, given Nigeria's imperfections, a call to citizenship and to a political and personal responsibility to the rebuilding of what has been lost.

The collection charts the memory trauma and the lingering effects of the Biafran-Nigerian Civil War, and the deep scars it has left on a whole generation, one to which I belong. The collection also traces multiple contexts and circumstances of the long-term implications of the initial loss of innocence, of trust, even of faith—as the poet attempts a new liturgy for self.

We see the depth and pain of that search in poems like "Memory: A Prayer," which opens:

> To remember is to reach into a fire
> to save a letter for you in a foreign tongue.

The constant human desire for meaning, for purpose, and the relentless pursuit of it, and the inevitable melancholy that attends our failure to obtain it, haunts this connection in profound ways that leave the reader shaken, affected but deeply grateful for the new insights it offers. In "What Is Not Remembered Is Not Redeemed," the poet says:

> What else is redemption if not love?
> A stare in the dark that has become a mirror.

What else indeed?

But in more than the general search for humanity, these poems contend with loss and exile in complex ways. From 1966 to 1970, Eze experienced, as did this writer, a war that took more than two million lives, including half a million children who died mostly of starvation. It cut an indelible wound into the psyche of the generation who fought it and our generation who survived it. Displaced and facing the worst ravages, Eze captures that unspeakable loss in the poem "The Exodus." The biblical reference here is also to the role the Catholic Church played in aid and the postwar coming of reggae as a musical form to help capture in poetry this loss.

> They turn their backs to their homes.
> They trek in a long line to nowhere.
> They do not look back. Seeing your home
> in flames turns you into a pillar of salt.

> In the foreground a boy has his shirt open.
> Behind him, another carries an empty tin.
> A lean woman has a basin full of her world.

In the poem "Our Eyes Are Watching God," there is a direct reference to that other genocide of Black Africans, slavery and its aftermath in America, and by extension the Zora Neale Hurston book. This kind of intertextuality between African writers and African American and even Caribbean writers is not new. The conversation of influence is perhaps better and easier seen and traced in music: enslaved West Africans bring music that in the Americas becomes the blues which is then taken back to West Africa by African American sailors in the early twentieth century who teach the chords to young Ghanaian dock boys who then turn it into Highlife which travels back to the New World becoming Soca and Calypso and reggae all of which come back to West Africa and influence juju and Afrobeat and so forth. It is sometimes harder to see in literature but it is there, even in the books of political purpose by early West African pro-independence politicians and activists, and we come to realize that there are no independence movements in West Africa without the movements first in the Caribbean, then in the United States. The fact is, the idea of a modern Africa owes as much to the African pioneers on the continent as it does to the Africans in the diaspora. It is the power of poetry, and, in particular, Eze's poetry, that this can be inferred by a title and the elegance of lines that allude to all this and yet also hold the existential angst and uneasiness we have toward easy answers and unresolvable pain and desire:

> They may be five and three, who can tell?
> Not from their stature. Nor from grayed hair.
> Skeletal heads,
> dappled lips;
> eyes,
> owls watching the sun.
>
> Are you the savior to come,
> or have you come to kill us?
>
> Our eyes are watching God.
> There's nothing else to look at
> when death stares at you.

So much of the political thrust of Eze's work is deeply rooted in a religious and spiritual ethical engagement. Perhaps a result of the Catholic faith of much of southern Igbo land and also Eze's own journey to faith, a faith he rejects in the priesthood but finds more dependably perhaps in the best ideals of human nature. In the poem "Remember Me," a woman acknowledges her own impending death from the sickness and hunger of war, and with no formal education and no access as a refuge to the accoutrement of writing, her body becomes the paper and her expression the ink, and yet her words are not of bitterness or even sadness but a reminder to lean into transformation, to make of the experience and suffering not a memory of loss but a watchword against ever losing humanity and returning to his depraved state of killing:

> Lacking pen and paper
> she makes her face
> an ancient papyrus
> for those who do not die.

> *Do not shed tears for me.*
> *Remember, decades form now,*
> *were weren't meant to live*
> *or die this way.*

It is from this established body of loss and experience that the poet turns his eye on others who suffer and suffered. By contending with his own personal and his culture's sense of loss and attempted redemption, he attempts to speak to and through other injustices perhaps as a way to resist the sentimental or to contend with the questions around an artist's right to lean into narratives not necessarily grounded in their own historical experience. We see this in "The Black Woman Killed by the Apartheid Police," a struggle and humble invocation found in lines like"

> It is love that made me speak for you.
> Forgive me if, in reading you,
> I thunder rather than whisper

This is not a protest, dear.
I remember you
to keep myself alive.

Or again in "The Nigerian Woman Who Was to Be Stoned for Making Love," where the poet writes a tender and intimate revelation of making love to a partner only to hear postcoital over the radio about the woman in Nigeria. There is no rage in his burn, no appropriation of another's experience or lack of power, no insertion of his own helplessness, but rather in lines like the ones below we see his power and his grace, an ability to implicate himself without ever making the narrative about him, without it ever being beyond reach, and which circles back from Nigeria to America and the lynch mobs of the South:

You, hands that hold stones,
what was it like to caress breasts?

If betrayed love could be cursed
in what language would it be?

Sad, like the tree in which
the innocent man hangs.

In this meditative and quietly lyrical approach, Chielozona Eze marks himself in this new African poetics not as a voice of easy protest, not as the voice of a bombast and rhetorical turn, but as the voice of an African poet in the twenty-first century trying to make sense of all the hunger, anger, war, loss, and desecration that has haunted his life and the lives of many Africans but remains always poised on that tender grace, that ease of dance, that transubstantiation that works an alchemy that is not about the outcome but always about the struggle, the engagement, and the terms thereof. Keorapetse Kgositsile, the South African poet of extraordinary humanness and distinction, would say, as he says gently and lovingly to many African artists, myself included, that Eze is a poet who carries our history with an easy grace.

Chielozona Eze means "May God not forget the king," or even better, "May the king never forget the destiny." This is the complication and deep beauty at the heart of this book. Eze has given us a deeply personal prayer and redemption, one strong enough to hand the hopes of the people on, and one that makes him a true and worthy successor of Christopher Okigbo.

prologue

Lagos, Lagos

Our plane broke through dense clouds
and glided over a sea of rusted roofs
               and skyscrapers
                    and slums
                         and palaces
                              and shanties
                              and refuse dumps
                              and people
                              and people.

Welcome to Lagos,
a city with a billion voices.
The beggar in the street who wished me Allah's love.
The street hawker who asked me to buy her *akara*.
The *molue* conductors, broken trumpets.
The muezzin who calls for prayer
and a street preacher sure the Lord comes tomorrow.

Lagos is not a place; it's a way of being:
you begin a phrase in Yoruba,
clause it in Edo, sentence it in Hausa,
and for color, add Igbo and English
– it all goes down the ear tube
like *edikaikong* down the throat.

It's not the Tower of Babel, my dear friend.
It's who we are. Our story.

How could I not love this city of twenty million heads?

And millions more in-between cracks,
too busy to be counted
always on the move
like humanity itself.

The three patriarchs

After the statue of three men, depicting Nigeria's three major ethnicities, the Hausa, the Igbo, and the Yoruba, lifting Nigeria.

Rivers Niger and Benue meet in Lokoja
and, murmuring in Esperanto,
rumble towards the Atlantic,
parting the land into three heavy chunks.

I think of the fallopian tubes and a vast uterus,
out of which Nigeria emerged,
stuttering in three languages,
underneath which are many others
it never paid heed to.

The three lifters' shoulders must be aching
under the weight of the colossal colony.
I'm left with a question every child would ask.
Isn't a stool studier with more legs than three?
I ask not as a student of politics
but of simple geometry.

the war survivor returns to his mother

The art of loving what is not perfect

My mother loves Saint Anthony,
the patron of lost things,
including me who came back
after years of exile in the West.

You're still the same, she said.
Like all sons in their moms' hearts, I thought.

But I've learned in humble ways:
I'm not the genius she said I was.
Nor did I become the rich man she'd hoped to see.
I'm her son, nonetheless, bruised and tempered

by clement and inclement weathers,
by loving and unloving strangers.

I learned from the worms
to wend my way in wet and dirt.
I know that any day could be the end.
Until then, good Lord, I trudge on, I,

an unfinished poem, tweaks here and there,
and hopes it will one day give a stranger a smile.

A look from the window of his old room

I looked from the window of my old room.
Two black wings spread out at the tree top.
A dark cloth rose and swung swiftly away.
And I thought: *like me years, years ago.*
I, too, had perched here for a long while.
The dreary village dawns, ghostly dusks.
My people, men and women, boastful lots
who thought the moon shone just for them.
I had believed fate fixed me as stars are to the ether.
For far too long, I heeded the words of my father:
Hold still, son. Listen! People had tried it in the past.
Where are they now? How did their story end?
The airplane impaled mile after mile.
A flying spider, it knitted countries to countries,
and my heart to uncommon fates.
I'm not Icarus. I didn't fall into the sea.
I refused to forget the hunger that chased me away
nor the broken people who haunted my peace.
To them I return with a bagful of stories
and nothing but open palms and itching ears.

Memory: a parable

I know a thing about memory:
It is a blind dog left in a distant city.
It finds a home in a shelter, waiting for love.
Months on, chance brings its master around.
At the sound of his voice it jumps and barks
and whines and wags its tail.
Will the master reject it again?

But memory is not a dog.
It's a cat:
stubborn,
clingy,
quiet,
purring beside you
even while you're on Facebook or WhatsApp
or while you watch Nigeria play Brazil.

Memory is a flea
that loves you
because you are alive.

I pluck you, flea, from behind my ear.
I do not throw you away to the dust.
I hold you before my eyes
to remind me I am a mere mortal.

Memory: a prayer

To remember is to reach into a fire
to save a letter for you in a foreign tongue.
You could be burnt again if it's translated.

I let words, spoken with pain,
bear witness to lives, lived.
I whisper them and pretend
the dead aren't dead.

What's human without memory?
What's memory that cannot heal?

Christ have mercy on the youth
who has never hugged a virgin on earth,
but hopes for seventy-two in heaven.
Christ have mercy on me,
who mistook war songs for love songs.

We went to war swearing to defeat the world.
We returned, sad that the world abandoned us.

Years on, did our wounds heal?
Or did they grow numb coatings?
How could I ever forget the silent groans,
or the many unheard prayers,
I, who saw Medusa's face and lived?

What's human without memory?
What's memory that cannot heal?

Warehouse of the past,
teach me not how evil others were to me;
teach me what I need to do

to be among the redeemed
who wrote on their ancestral walls:

*The past, if forgotten, pollutes
the village drinking well.*

What is not remembered is not redeemed

Not long ago, I walked into a bar in my village.
I said to the barmaid, *give me two shots of ogogoro*
to calm the bubbles of my undigested meal.
On the other side of the counter
boys of my town sang of war
and of a new world to be born of pain.
And I shook my head and said to myself
Poor kids, nursed with the milk of denial.
If only they knew, we too had sung of war
and marched off to the front, armed with naked zeal.
Only the lucky ones came back home with broken legs
and broken minds. Many others did not return.
I had sworn to the gods above and below,
if I made it back alive and whole, I'd love
the birds that sing even when no one listens.
What else is redemption if not love?

                              A stare
                              in the dark
that has become a

                              mirror.

he looks at the pictures of the war he survived

Unknown boy soldiers

After the picture of bare-chested youths doing parade with
pieces of wood in place of guns

I take out a pack of pictures from my drawer
and this is what I see:

Teenage boys with skeletal chests pumped.
White pieces of wood rest on their bony collars
like elephant tusks.

I think of the Chinese Terra-cotta warriors.
Pawns, they, too, swore an oath to their emperor.
Did they know their cause?

This earth, my brothers - If only they had known
They'd lose their lives, bones bleached.
in the bushes of the fatherland.
No stones nor sons to bear their names.

The exodus

After the picture of people fleeing the Biafran War

They turn their backs to their homes.
They trek in a long line to nowhere.
They do not look back. Seeing your home
in flames turns you into a pillar of salt.

In the foreground a boy has his shirt open.
Behind him, another carries an empty tin.
A lean woman has a basin full of her world.
Girls, girls, boys, girls, women, women.

I know the first boy forgot his toy in the backyard.
I'm the other boy dreaming of the moon left behind.
in the village. I see the elderly woman in the midst
and I hear grandma's questions resound from years ago:

Why?
Where are we going?
When shall we be back?
Why?

Our eyes are watching God
After the picture of two children on the front cover of 1968
Life Magazine titled, "Starving Children of Biafra War"

They may be five and three, who can tell?
Not from their size.
Nor from grayed hair,
skeletal heads,
dappled lips,
eyes,
owls
watching the sun.

Are you the savior to come
or have you come to kill us?

Our eyes are watching God.
There's nothing else to look at
when death looks at you.

Starved girl
After the picture of a kwashiorkor child sitting on a table,
titled "Starved Girl"

The ground is dirt.
Grasses are in spots.
A white wall darkens
two children on a wobbly table.
The one faces the camera.
The other stares at the ground.
Her ribs jut out,
her belly balls forth.
Thinning limbs, bloated feet.
Walking must be hell.

If you listen well you can hear me whisper:
Merciful God,
why are we doing this to ourselves?

Boy with a kwashiorkor belly

After the picture of a boy with kwashiorkor belly lying in a bed

Lying in a cot is a boy.
An upturned frog.

In the sea of whiteness
his belly is a dark globe.
How did he swallow a football?

You can hear his prayer,
or perhaps a curse
or a word of caution:
deal with what you see.

Before death, hell
After the picture of hungry people surrounding a relief vehicle
for food

Men and woman surround a white Land Rover.
Toddlers cling to their mothers as to life.
Three steps from them
as if from love,
closer to the camera
as to eternity
a child crouches,
all bones and ribs,
abandoned,
supporting his head
with his left hand,
unable to stand up
for his own relief, food
which might have arrived late.
Too late.

I've heard preachers say that hell comes after death.
But I've been in hell thirty months long.
And I've learned to love the earth, imperfect as it is,
thirty times better than the promise of heaven.

The shame of empty plates
*After the picture of a woman in front of a Red Cross vehicle
waiting for food*

She wedges her bony child on her left hip,
supports him with her left arm
clutching an empty plate.
She balances a basket on her head
as if held with a glue.
By her right a Red Cross truck unloads.
Behind her a child holds out an empty plate.

I've known the shame of empty plates.
I've known the sadism of slow death
that kills the soul and leaves the body
to coast along
a few more days
or weeks
like an airplane that has ran out of fuel.

If I refuse to let go of this shame, dear heaven,
it is to remember to love every human
the way my mother taught me do.

Always.

Remember me
After the picture of a haggard woman who sits in front of her house waiting for death

She makes it out the door.
Her thighs are stockfish.
Her stomach is a sad balloon.
Beside her is a long broom
to shoo unruly flies
impatient for her spirit to move on.
She knows it'll not be long.
A couple more days, or just a week.

Lacking pen and paper
she makes her face
an ancient papyrus
for those who survive:

Do not shed tears for me.
Remember years from now,
we weren't meant to live
or die this way.

he talks with his memory

He who has no sin

How easy it is, Good Lord,
to cast   stones
at adulterous women everywhere.

You know I'm not innocent.
I, who would have loved to take a chance
with one of them in the dark.

Have mercy on me for slinging a shot at my enemies.
I, who, am no better than them.
But for the grace of questions that wash up
on my mind like dead fishes on the shore,
there go I the path of the king's hangman.

Letter to self from a city that survived

On reading Afam Akeh, "Letter Home."

Dear friend,
I write to let you know I'm alive.
I'm not the only one who survived.
But many others have sworn never to look back.
The ruins of the past scare them to death.
We have birthed a new breed of kids
who are addicted to quick pleasure,
who call our stories of defeat fake news
and so gulp the same old wine of folly
from new wineskin.
Our heroes have forgotten the feel of pain.
They, who spoke truth to power,
now feed power to their truth.
I write to let you know I've parted ways with the tribe
that has no pile of stone or a cove for their dead.
But I'd be damned if I reject
the people who taught me to sing,
gods, who through toil and pain
turned clay into humans.
Fresh off the wombs, we burst into a yodel
to free the chest of choke.
We have never ceased to sing since then.
Not even when ears are turned away from us.

Memory, again

Those who want to see light
as it is
must retire
into the shadow.
- Hans Magnus Enzensberger, "Shadow Realm."

O memory,
sometimes I see your face in a fog
like a temptress in veil.
Sometimes I hear your roar in the distance
like a jet lost in the clouds.
Sometimes I perceive you like the scent of the girl
who taught me to love.

How could I not love this muddled water,
Spiritus Mundi?

It is not cowardice that shooed me
into the shadow of the past.
I am the arrow in a taut bow,
ready to snap.

But I am a crooked arrow,
in search of self.

Always. Always. Always.

How did the song end?

I'm back to the small hill
on which we sang war songs, and boasted
to wrestle the enemy with our bare knuckles.

The small hill is still silent.
As always. Like the moon
and the stars. And days and nights.

Oh fatherland.
We trusted you knew where we were going.
We trusted you knew what we were doing.

How did the song end, dear God?
What questions have you got for us?
We, who believed to know more than you do.

Speak to me, memory

My tongue turned numb
when I saw a man struck by a bomb.
He opened his mouth.
I did not hear what came out.

When my tongue came to life years later
I swore never to utter
truths in the language of cherubs
or the shibboleths of the celebs.

I learned to speak like little kids.
And I say what I read on his lips
before his last fight
Boy, run for your life.

There is no other.
Not here. Not after.

Ode to my refugee shirt

My favorite shirt survived our war,
but with tears and holes here and there.
I couldn't discard it, for I had no better one
so, I took it to our village seamstress.
Her Singer treadle machine did not work.
Never mind, she said, *mending is better done with own hands*
just like your mother cared for you when you were this small.
She cupped her hands to show how small I used to be.
Just keep your eyes on the needle and thread.
There are many ways to mend clothes like this.
For these minor tears I'll stitch in little suns,
stars or flowers, something to please the eye.
For this bigger hole, I'll put a pocket.
A pocket anywhere is for the unknown.
Three days later I came back for my shirt.
She held it to me, face all smiles. *You see,* she said.
Everything that is rent can be mended with care.

Not letting the dead bury the dead

In that small garden behind our house
there were two army boots and a helmet
with three holes, three windows to see heaven's backyard.
I thought the boots were gifts from above.
But my mother didn't think so: *Bring no curse
on your head, son,* she said.
And muttering some prayers, she buried them there.

Decades have now passed.
The war lies in the past.
Like my trophy, buried in our garden.
I dug them up one day, tilling that soil for vegetable.

I refused to bury them once again.
They should lie around,
stick out like an accusing finger.
Let the ghost of the owner roam the earth,
and the rest of us coast along,
war orphans, who have forgotten
what made them limp rather than walk.

The human condition

We were fleeing our refugee camp under a bomb attack.
A boy with snotty nose ran back for his people.
O my dear, where were they?
How did their story end?

My father said to me on his deathbed:
I leave behind nothing but words.
Hold them like children do their birthday gifts.
Let go if they hurt.

I seek no more mysteries in life.
Nor do I indulge in the trickeries of words.
I hold on to this simple words of the ages:
Civilization is an elastic rubber band

it stretches as long as you hold tight.
If you let go, it comes back with a bite

In praise of question marks

A question mark is a mirror in a mist,
potent for its haziness.
A question mark is a fishing hook
that wants to walk.
? ?

I throw you, lovely hook,
into a murky river.
You might catch a fat fish.
Or perhaps a sad toad.
If you come up with nothing, dear hook,
I'll still take you home.
I'll hang you by my window frame.
And when I look out to the world,
I see requests wrongly made.
I see finitude, mirror of my face.

Stocktaking

After Natasha Trethewey, "Bookkeeping"

These are the things to remember:
my jutting ribs, bloating feet,
yellowing cheeks, graying hair,
a pair of rivulets on my father's cheeks,
and my mother's whisper to God to still hold on.

Of what use is it to take stock
of what we ate or did not eat
and that we nearly died from both?

After the war, we had dance on our feet.
Songs gurgled from our parched throats:
hurrah, war is no more, war has been won.
My father drank to forget he ever cried.
Why recall what puts you to shame, he said.
But then we began our own war
that ate us from within, inch after inch
like worms the barn.

We fought the war that begins
after others have ended.

How to survive wars that survive

After the sound of the last gun had left our ears
and bombs fell no more,
after we had patched the wounds on the walls
and healed the holes in the roofs,
after we had made fire to chase away some lurking ghosts,
after we had drunk water from our wells
and lived to drink again;
when we were sure we had survived,
we began to tell stories to thrive.
We were well aware of the ancient wisdom:
After the civil war
comes the unseen war that only love
and songs can win.

Praying for the weak in times of endless wars

I rejoiced when the children of my town said to me:
uncle, tell us the story of how you survived the war,
how you disappeared your waterbelly for good.
I left Amokwe in your age, dear friends.
Thirty months on, I was rained and sunned in strange jungles
of Igboland. I came back grayed like a bald eagle
with a voice stubborn as a bedbug: *Was it worth it?*

Oh Christ, friend of Lazarus,
bring back my childhood joys
from the jungles of pipedream.
But I've not come to point fingers
I lost them all thirty times over.
But look at my arms: long and wide for the world.
And even when I hug myself
I always leave
              a space
                      in between
for the unknown.
How else can we survive new wars of all against the weak?

Picking mushrooms

My mother's first act when we returned from the refugee
camps:
Gather us around her favorite picture of Virgin Mary
with the child Jesus on her lap. *She protected us*, she said.

A week on, I went with Grandma to our village shrine.
She, too, had her ways to explain our survival.
We thank the gods who brought you back to me, she said.

What could I say?
What did I know about pictures and masks and statues?
Yet I prayed to all the gods, living or dead, native or foreign.

To them I said: *You who could not defeat the enemies,
do me this one simple favor*:
Turn my world of pain into a gain for the world.

The color of money

Like all postwar boys, I picked bullet shells
in hopes they held some wealth.
I picked them in the village square,
and in the nearby bushes
and in school yards,
even beside the church.
I filled up an empty tin of Peak milk
happy I was good at that game.
I would hold each shell tight in my fist
like I used to hold a Nigerian nickel
with a hole in the middle,
a star around the hole,
the British king over it all.
Bullets and money had the same color.
The Biafran war taught me so.
Everyday, I looked into my treasure tin.
Every year they turned greener,
the color I thought life meant.
But out of copper comes no life.
And now, many years gone
I look back with wild wonder,
troubled by the ghosts of the unburied
and the questions we failed to ask.

Refusing my father's fate

Finally I just gave up and became my father -
Sharon Olds, "Fate"

I couldn't avoid his discreet gnash of teeth
and his slumped shoulders of defeat.
He pulled them up in a lightning speed
when he thought I had seen him in need.

I didn't see as much as he had seen,
but what I saw made me cringe in shame.
Like him, I prayed to rather be blind
than see humans devour their own kind.

Finally I just gave up and became my father
but I refused to drink and curse the other.
I feared I would take my defeat on my wife
whose fault, like that of my mother

was that she married a man broken by war.
I refused the evil I saw in the day
to stare back at me in the dark of the night.
I refuse the pain I've suffered to be my blight.

Epiphany

We were walking down the village path one evening.
My friend tapped at my shoulder and said: *Look, our veteran!*
But I only saw his back, the icicles of his tattered shirt
caressing the bumps of his bare buttocks.

Maybe he didn't want to shame us with his naked front
and the accusing flickers from his eyeballs.
Our myths still echo with his exploits:
how he practiced with a dumb gun and slew Goliaths.

He walked into the bush where he had made himself a hut
and left us to deal with our silence.
We, who have forgotten all about them
for they no longer wear the clothes we made for them.

God shows himself in the twilight
so that each person could retire in the dark
to eavesdrop on the truth that whispers
when the noise of the day has died.

he remembers other people in pain

The black woman killed by the apartheid police *

> Around the pelvis is a blue plastic bag. 'Oh, yes,' the
> grave indicator remembers. 'We kept her naked and
> after ten days she made herself these panties … she
> was brave.'
>
> – Antjie Krog, *Country of my Skull*

To know how things stand we unearth.
Piece by piece, from the heap of bones,
the narrative lifts us from the ash of silence.

We're judged by the stories we tell.
But only the dead know the truth,
they who speak to us in silence.

I speak of you not to judge the enemy.
I speak to you out of love to you
who refused to give up your honor.

I put into notes the groans of the many
who still live like mongrels in slums,
the many, whose panties are torn,

who are raped like the land before them.
It is love that made me speak for you.
Forgive me if, in reading you,

I thunder rather than whisper.
This is not a protest, dear.
I remember you
to keep myself alive

* During the South African Truth and Reconciliation Commission, the
remains of the victims of apartheid police brutality were unearthed to help
the commission determine the extent of the crimes of the past.

The Nigerian woman who was to be stoned for making Love

For Amina Lawal*

For lovemaking, my woman likes music in the background.
After some dancing around with words,
some sweet shy glances and smiles,
I hold her hands and kiss the nape of her neck
and she says *wait a second* and lets the music set play.
In our early days, we shared a cigarette afterward.
But I no longer smoke, and rather than stay in silence,
she tells me some minor stories, like the type of cloth
I wore when she first saw me.
Like what I said, or did not say that won her over.
I had forgotten all those little things.
But I will never forget the joy of the first night.
Nor that of yesterday that came without rituals,
like a warm summer rain.
I gave her no time to put on her music,
and later we listened to the radio.
Somewhere in Northern Nigeria a woman would be stoned
for making love to a man.
I looked my woman in the eye.

Silence.
Like the shape of guilt.
You, hands that hold stones,
what was it like to caress breasts?
If betrayed love could be cursed
in what language would it be?
Sad, like the tree in which
the innocent man hangs.

*Amina Lawal, a Nigerian Muslim woman, was sentenced to death by stoning in 2002 by a Sharia court for adultery. The death sentence was later overturned after international protests.

Victuals for the Dead

For Gloria Eze, 1973 – 2005

I know a small hill down the village road
where the dead come to meet daily at dawn.
I went there for you; you couldn't be found.
Did we bury you so deep into our gluey loam?

What pried you from us is stronger than our will
but what binds us is tougher than the pull of death.
I offer you these words as victuals on your way.
Take them and do not look back in regret.

Since you never visited us I know you're loved
wherever you are the way we've loved you.
What else could have rent our hearts as your death did?
I speak to you not to make you feel guilty;

I speak to you to let you know and have you beam:
In every corner of our house I find silky threads
of your hearty laugh; they stitch our hearts back again
to the shape that love has meant them to be.

An elegy

*For Kofi Awoonor (1935-2013), Ghanaian poet, who
was killed by Islamic terrorists while he was
attending a poetry festival in Nairobi, Kenya,
September 21, 2013.*

I do not ask whether these new tears make a difference.
I do not wonder how much ache my soul can take.

He was a gentle soul who would sing rather than curse.
He was a careful hand that would mold rather than punch.

I've never been to the land that flows with milk and honey,
but I know how milk and honey are made.

And I knew a bee whose wings carried it far ashore
and, loaded with nectar, back to its dome, built,

block after block to shield the sweetness of its sweat.
And if cruel boys or girls have to swat it dead

would it rather not die working for the Promised Land,
making honey, more honey in place of hate?

A new planting season

For Chinua Achebe – 1930-2013

Before his last breath the elder showed his hands,
palm up. *Empty*, he said, *like the long road ahead.*
I've planted the seeds my father put in them;
planted them the way my mother taught me.

Look around you and in the old barn.
More seeds, dung, watering cans, machetes,
two sided machetes. What needed to be said
has been said. Everything else is up to you.

Of gods, love and grandma

When I turned nineteen, a friend gave me
a mini-radio, silvery, glinting at every twirl.
I sat under an orange tree in front of our house,
listened to a story, laughed now and then.

My Grandma asked why I was so amused.
Poseidon was the Greek god of the sea, I said.
Like other gods, he raped the girls of Arcadia.
The way he did to Medusa in Athena's temple.

Athena turned away from the evil, but punished
Medusa, changed her hair to revolting snakes.
Grandma did not turn away her face;
she merely asked: *Is that a reason to laugh?*

But that was years ago. Grandma is dead.
Many wars have been fought,
many more women and girls have been raped.
Leaves have yellowed, reddened, fallen.

Everything will pass away, I know,
but not Grandma's voice and calm brown eyes,
deep, with many stories yet to be told,
many questions yet to be answered.

In search of my father's dreams

The other day in the town's arena,
a man asked why I carried a placard
against wars and hate, and the rape of girls.
Why did I shout like a noisy punk?

Of war and peace, friend, I've got this to say:
My father died with half a dream in his eyes.
Years on I still tap in the dark for the other half.
He once told me in a tone of defeat:

If only I had gone to school I wouldn't be this poor.
But God knows why he was poor,
why he woke up mornings with tears
and whispered: *never again, never again.*

I've been through the school of pain, dear friend.
I'm not the one that speaks when I speak;
thousand tongues meld in my mouth.
For them I demand an answer.

My eyes search every corner for the other half
of my father's dream. I'll know it when I see it.
Conceived in the dark night of fear,
it will find me in the open arena of daylight

where children
       dream
             with eyes wide
                     open.

An army roadblock

It was about noon at the roadblock where
two students died a year ago. The soldiers reeked
of sweat and liquor. I raised my eyes to the sky.
There must be stars to bear witness.

If I could tell the soldiers how I felt,
I'd say I'm the first of Congolese workers,
whose hands were cut off by King Leopold II.
But they'd say: we're not wicked white people.

Or, I would tell them I'm like Steve Biko
beaten to death by the apartheid police.
But they'd say: apartheid is history, man,
we're now Africans among Africans.

Or, I would tell them I'm an ugly spider
that devours its guts out of self-spite.
But they'd say: you don't look like a spider;
you're a Nigerian man acting white.

But I'd tell them I'm not acting white,
I only dream of a decent life without
humiliations, life that doesn't force me to tears
like it often did to my mother whom

I drove to the city weeks ago and who said:
There's a war going on. And I said:
No, mama the war ended long time ago.
But then she asked: *Why do they point guns at us?*

I had no answer then. Nor do I have one now.
Like her I hope it's true that he who lives

by the sword shall not die by own sword,
but live long to tell of his haunted dreams.

he just wants to dance

Regrets of a crippled veteran - folksong

Amam gboo jebe ami
Wunyee m'akanutago,
amam gboo jebe ami
Ndi nkuzi elibe ugwo,
amam gboo jebe ami
ndi oloko elibe ugwo
amam gboo jebe ami
ndi boys etebe egwu
amam gboo jebe ami

Had I known I wouldn't have gone to war.
The wife I would have married.
Had I known I wouldn't have gone to war.
Teachers now receive monthly salaries.
Had I known I wouldn't have gone to war.
The rail workers now receive salaries.
Had I known I wouldn't have gone to war.
Boys now dance the newest dance.
Had I known I wouldn't have gone to war.

Could he haunt others as he was haunted?

… but then
when darkness falls over us all
and we cower
        or coil
        into ourselves like fetuses
or, like house hens,
put our heads close to our chests
and hear frenzied beats,
we will answer to our names
to know when we lost that line,
that sifts hearts from stones.

And I search again in the ruins of our youths.
Perhaps, there'll be a thing to find,
ordinary stones we pretend are pearls.

He celebrates his 50th birthday

After Mary Oliver, "In Blackwater
Woods."

I've long learned to make peace with my mirror:
the deepening lines on my face,
the blanched hair on my balding head
like errant plume on an egg.
I do not speak of the cracks of bones in the mornings,
nor the pinch and pain in the joints.

I know the joy of life after death.
A gift the gods make to very few.

I've learned to love this earth, mortal as it is
like orgasm
to be sought after
for its shortness
like everything real.

Whatever evil I had suffered, I forget

> *Whatever evil I had suffered, I forget*
> *Czeslaw Milosz, "Gift."*

The migrant birds sing to the dying sun
though they know darkness is on the horizon.
Isn't that why they are light, carried by the wind
across mountains and seas, across boundaries?

Fired up, I want my grim-faced God to know
today he has lost one more bowing head.
I pity the praying voice,
who called for blood in the name of justice.

Why should I gnash my teeth this late in my age?
Why should I grouse that I suffered starvation
and had been in the crosshair of executioners?
Whatever evil I had suffered, I forget.

I hold on to the goodness I've seen
and recall with a feminine mind:
I'm alive, I'm alive.
And I toast to this hour

and I sing to shed more weight
till I am one with the air,
one with the eternal giving
out of which we all came.

Survival kit

The boy said: Take my right eye,
It has seen too much, but leave me the left.
I will need it to see God
– Chris Abani, "Say Something about Child's Play"

… but then, they took our left eyes,
for they said only they should see God.

They're all gone,
pouches heavy with our blood.

We're finding ways to lend one another blood.
That, dear friend, is how we've learnt to survive.

And we hold on to these stories,
these songs.

And we smile to ourselves
as we watch God feel his way
to our kitchen table.

The traveler

Ojemba enwe ilo - a traveler has no enemy – Igbo proverb

For your journey,
choose a bag as big as the world.
Remember it's going to be long.
Put in a feather and a scoop of soil.
How could you do without a god?
But when strangers ask you which
god you've brought along
show them your palms,
empty, blank, open to give or take.
Do not forget to put in many stories,
you'll need them for the children of the foreign land.
And when there is no one to listen
speak to the wind and pretend you're not alone.

You are,
      indeed,
        never
           alone.

Sitting on an egg

So All the Time I Was Sitting on an Egg
- Lola Shoneyin

Poetry is an egg.
It's nothing without the care
of a brooding parent, the warmth of life.
It's nothing without shells that ward off critters.

Eggs are always a mystery.
They give birth to singers and stingers;
ones with fangs of poison,
others with wings of passion.

I, too, sit on an egg
hoping that what comes out
will have wings
even if it doesn't fly.

As a child I had a pet hen that never flew.
Now and again, though, it tried.
And I knew it never forgot what wings are for.

When poetry heals

The voices that hive to my ears.
The many ears I seek to whisper to.

I write poems to stay young
and sane:
when the preacher shouts to save the world
when the rapper curses the good and the bad
when neighbor's dog barks till dawn
when politicians spew hyperboles and hatred.

I eavesdrop on the silence,
lost in the cracks of words.
The breath of a comma.

Printed in the United States
By Bookmasters